The Travels of Blad J. Garamond

In Search of Geneviève Sans-Serif

The Travels of Blad J. Garamond

In Search of Geneviève Sans-Serif

Selections from the Poetical Memoirs of the Last Living Descendant of Claude Garamond, Typesetter, with Miscellaneous Reflections on His Adventures, &c.

Edited with Commentary by the Author's Faithful Assistant.

Austin Allen

Measure Press
Savannah, Georgia

Printed in the United States of America
First Edition

Composition by R.G.
Manufacturing by Ingram.

Allen, Austin
The Travels of Blad J. Garamond / by Austin Allen — 1st ed.

ISBN-13: 978-1-939574-41-1
ISBN-10: 1-939574-41-2
Library of Congress Control Number: 2025945609

Measure Press
2 Longberry Lane
Savannah, GA 31419

http://www.measurepress.com/measure/

Acknowledgements

Blad's voyage to publication has taken over fifteen years. I'm grateful to everyone who helped along the way.

Thanks, first of all, to Measure Press editors Paul Bone and Rob Griffith for giving this book a home, and to my friend Lisa Perrin for her wonderful cover art. Many thanks, too, to Chris Childers, Jenna Lê, and Claire Wahmanholm for providing blurbs and other kind support.

My gratitude to the fellow writers who've read the manuscript at various stages, including Brian Brodeur, Abigail Deutsch, Boris Dralyuk, Joey Frantz, Jenna Lê, Shane McCrae, Leanna Petronella, Katherine Robinson, Matthew Buckley Smith, Ryan Wilson, and Erica Wright. Special thanks to Matthew for steering this manuscript toward Measure, and to Ryan for publishing an excerpt in *Literary Matters.*

Thanks to my former Abbeville Press coworkers Erin Dress, Briana Green, Lauren Evangelista, Megan Malta, and Michaelann Millrood for supporting this project in its earliest phase; Douglas Basford, Caki Wilkinson, and David Yezzi for indulging Blad's antics later in his development; and the Bowery Poetry Club for hosting two Garamond performances.

I'm indebted to many friends and former colleagues at the University of Cincinnati — particularly Emily Rose Cole, Caitlin Doyle, John Drury, and Rebecca Lindenberg — for their generosity as readers. I'm also lucky to have received material support from the University of Cincinnati, Johns Hopkins University, the Poetry by the Sea conference, and the Sewanee Writers' Conference.

Finally, this book is dedicated to my wife Porscha, without whose love, wisdom, and encouragement it would not exist.

On with the voyage.

For Porscha

CONTENTS

I. PREPARATIONS

II. SETTING FORTH

III. WANDERLUST

IV. INTERLUDE

V. TROUBLE WITHIN TROUBLE

VI. SOUVENIRS

Begin with an individual, and before you know it you find that you have created a type; begin with a type, and you find that you have created — nothing.

— *F. Scott Fitzgerald, "The Rich Boy"*

[Galliard] possesses an authentic sparkle that is lacking in the current Garamonds. The italic is particularly felicitous and reaches back to the feeling...from which Claude Garamond's italic departed.

— *Printer's colophon,* Anatomy of a Typeface, *Alexander Lawson*

In this strange Labyrinth how shall I turne...

— *Lady Mary Wroth, "A Crown of Sonnets Dedicated to Love"*

Dandyism, an institution outside the law, has a rigorous code of laws that strictly binds all its subjects, however ardent and independent their characters may be.

— *Charles Baudelaire, "The Dandy"*

The only true exile is the writer who lives in his own country.

— *Julio Cortázar*

To bring a lover, a lady and a rival into the fable; to entangle them in contradictory obligations, perplex them with oppositions of interest, and harass them with violence of desires inconsistent with each other; to make them meet in rapture and part in agony; to fill their mouths with hyperbolical joy and outrageous sorrow; to distress them as nothing human ever was distressed; to deliver them as nothing human ever was delivered, is the business of a modern dramatist. For this probability is violated, life is misrepresented, and language is depraved.

— *Samuel Johnson, "Preface to Shakespeare"*

I

PREPARATIONS

EDITOR'S PREFACE

The Travels of Blad J. Garamond *is an epic memoir in progress. The author needs no further introduction than the rumors you've already heard. Nor does Mme Sans-Serif, to whom his efforts here are dedicated. Embarking on the project and his latest journey, he sent me this note:*

> I will tell my story in verse because my life is poetry, and in serial form because my life is ongoing.
>
> Installments will be irregular and posted in dispatches from around the globe. Their ordering will be altered, or not, by the vagaries of international mail. The text will be fragmentary owing to sharks, rapier thrusts, and revision.
>
> Please publish each installment with a mimimum of prefatory explanation. I trust you as my public trusts me. Their curiosity has reached a fever pitch: I aim to satisfy.
>
> B.J.G.

DRAMATIS PERSONAE

[Repurposed from the libretto of Mr. Garamond's abandoned operetta. — Ed.]

BLADWELL JAMES GARAMOND IV

Globetrotter, gambler, connoisseur, collector,
paramour, dabbler, duelist, bibliophile.
Fond of the Windsor knot, the Oxford comma,
the impromptu cocktail and the opportune remark
made simultaneously. Esteemed director
of amateur theatricals in Garamond Park,
which showcase the American flair for drama
that has sustained him through his long exile.
Thirty-nine-year-old bachelor. Believes
pipe smoking is a virtue, not a vice,
and finds that ladies find its halo nice.
Blends in a pinch of opium when he grieves.

GENEVIÈVE SANS-SERIF

Equestrian, cosmologist, cinephile, spy.
Black velvet. Garnet bracelet. Gimlet eye.
Commands the tongues of nearly all the nations.
Slender but strong, reserved but not aloof.
Dark hair, deft fingers. Smile a shorthand proof
of all you've left out of your calculations.
Speaks fluent *mot juste*, phrases blazing but
clipped, silver lighter flipped
open, flipped
shut.

THE RIVAL

Said to be handsome. Skilled, one must admit,
at swordplay. Part-time lawyer. Full-time shit.

Also featuring:

An EDITOR.
An ANCESTOR.
Four PARENTS.
A HORSE.
A SCHOLAR.
A VENDOR.
An ASTRONOMER.
The SEA.

II

SETTING FORTH

AU VOYAGE

She left me in style. Absconded in the night.
Hopped into a gondola — I mean the kind
hot-air balloons have (but this *was* in Venice) —

flourished a knife and cut the mooring ropes.
She touched her Gauloise to the pilot light,
bailed out the blue sheath of her evening gown…

I ran up panting, shouting: “Lunch tomorrow?”
She blew a kiss. “You’ve got to be realistic.”
I watched her float away, nude over the roofs,

and felt the city sink another inch.

L'ORIGINE DU GARAMOND

"To be born"
is to be fatally passive — I débuted.

In Central Park. The back of a cab. Horse-drawn,
of course: steed rearing, driver clutching his hat
and waxing pale. His coattails flecked with blood.
The vendor of salted nuts offering his tongs
as forceps. Father laboring to appear
composed as Mother groaned: "Not here, not here!"

She meant America. It wasn't *that*
godawful as a place to take a trip —
but as a claim upon my citizenship?
She'd almost rather see me cleft in two…
Yet she let go. The driver swooned. The steed
stood still. The vendor held me high; the throngs
greeted my vocal warm-ups with a cheer.

I had arrived — a bit before my cue —
but Mother swore we'd never travel *there* again.
Soon I was flying back at breathless speed
in dreams: drawn homeward, homeward, without halt…
At five I begged, "Can't *I* go? I'm American!"
She laughed and turned away. "That's not my fault."

L'ORIGINE II: ANCESTRY

The types that currently bear the name of the great sixteenth-century punchcutter Claude Garamond...do not always have the same characteristics, a disconcerting factor that interferes with their ready identification.

— Alexander Lawson, *Anatomy of a Typeface*

I am descended from *the* Garamond.
My line springs from the foundry of his loins.

The man, the myth, the font.
Born "Garamont"
(the name was altered by a later printer),

he published handsome books
and decked out French
with rakish accent marks and pirate hooks.
Also apostrophes. (Which turned possessive
only when pirated by Englishmen
around the time my family crossed the Channel.
In France, they just elide.)

Genealogy, the most regressive
pathway to family pride,
confirms my claim.
I am the last true Garamond. (I hear
Geneviève snort: *If that is your real name.*)

SKETCHES FROM CHILDHOOD

My first works: family portraits. Crayon mostly.
A burnt sienna series, a periwinkle cycle.

Father a dozen different shades of ghostly.
Dark bloodhound pouches under bloodshot eyes.
Vice chair of things: the London Stock Exchange,
the local cricket league. Himself a great
but thwarted batsman — blamed a wicked ankle
and an angled wicket. Prone to alternate
between brass-buttoned double-breasted suits
and utter self-neglect. Umber mustache
streaked silver, papers in his attaché
unstapled, undeciphered to this day.

Mother a ballroom dancer, radio engineer,
believer in broad hats and vermilion scarves.
Stopped at one child for the sake of her career,
then had a career as fitful as her child.
Became a hobbyist. Built luminous-dialed
equipment in our den, kept one ear glued
to chatter from the Kremlin or from fishing wharves
or admirals who'd lost their latitude —
could someone please advise? *No clue*, she said.
Hummed them a long, slow, soothing waltz instead.

A sepia period … I drew our three
stiff figures side by side (me labeled ME)
in front of the splendid House of Garamond.

Balustrades, battlements, portico, koi pond.
The pair of chimneys whose designer flues
actually gave off smoke in curlicues.

A STRANGER APPEARS

One Friday in the backyard labyrinth
where I'd sneak off to smoke my father's pipe
and hide from school, a girl I'd never seen
peeked through a door — I hadn't seen that either —
beckoned, retreated down the aisles of green,
and led me to a white horse streaked by weather.
An equine statue, limestone, riderless.
She mounted to the bare back from the plinth
and stared straight at me. *You are coming up, or — ?*
Blankly I nodded, followed, let her hold
my hand as our legs dangled, let her press
her lips' soft print to mine … Her face was bold,
style plain and elegant …
I'd found my type.
(Found her. Or she'd found me.) Then off she went —
hopped down and left me wandering toward supper.

A visitor, the child of dignitaries
(our threshold in those days was graced by many):
mother a crystallographer, father a diplomat.
They visited more often after that.
The grownups in the parlor, sipping sherries,
gossiped about electrons or the Bourse
or my poor grades, as I slipped off with "Genny"
into a hedge or cupola to play.
A new nook every time. Needless to say,
we never found our way back to that horse.

EXPERIMENT

But I who have taken happiness both in a solid and liquid shape...who have conducted my experiments upon this interesting subject with a sort of galvanic battery, and have, for the general benefit of the world, inoculated myself, as it were, with the poison of 8,000 drops of laudanum per day...I (it will be admitted) must surely know what happiness is, if anybody does.

— Thomas De Quincey,
Confessions of an English Opium-Eater

I was a well-bred boy in tailored velvet.
Most days I made my parents mostly proud.
But when I saw them pouring homemade cordial
at a soirée one night, I turned primordial.
That gleaming candy-colored stuff . . . I vowed
to hunt it down wherever they might shelve it.

I found the vial and went on a tear:
yanked out the stopper, took a rabid quaff,
belched, ran from corridor
to labyrinth to solarium and back, drank more,
cleaned out the after-dinner mints, whacked off
to dryad statuettes, puked in the urn,
pulled down the hanging gardens frond by frond,
set fire to model ships and watched them burn
and sink in the koi pond,
unleashed the hounds of the House of Garamond,
and landed in the lap of my au pair.

She hauled me off to bed, cursing in German.
The constellations on my ceiling spun…
Foretold in that fake glow I could determine
vaguely the shape of my first grown-up task:
to find out, vial by vial, flask by flask,
what is and isn't fun.

CONTACT

Every few nights
I crept down to the den,
switched on the panel full of dials and lights,
and found my girl again.

The frequency was secret, prearranged.
The pitch grew lower as our voices changed.

She sang:

> *Blad, Blad, don't be sad,*
> *We'll meet again before you know it.*
> *Blad, Blad, don't go mad,*
> *Although you say you are a poet.*
> *Blad, Blad, don't be bad.*
> *There is a line. Be sure to toe it.*

— *It's an expression, yes? "To toe the line"?*
It sounds so odd. I said it sounded fine,
or even beautiful, the way she said it.
Toh. Toh. I promised her I'd mind my mother,
bring up my grades, and generally bring credit
back to my name, so we could see each other.
(Her father'd made some noise about forbidding
contact between us, and he wasn't kidding.)

We'd sync our schedules via Swiss Chronometer
and eavesdrop on a planet at the tip

of the fourth arm of Andromeda,
straining to hear each crackle, hiss, and blip —
each local anomaly: a passing comet or
wayward ship, a pulsar's heartbeat-skip…

She'd take down notes, decode it all by dawn,
and, once she'd shared the juiciest gossip, yawn.

Blad, Blad, Blad.
Stay sweet. Do not be bad
with anyone but me.
Bisou bisou. Bonne nuit.

LINGUA FRANCA

Tutors in languages I still can't speak.
A hundred languages and no retention.
Tutors in Latin, French, and modern Greek
whose false teeth clenched at every failed declension;

classes in Finnish, which I halfway mastered;
courses in Catalan and Portuguese,
which my brain blent into one splendid bastard;
Mandarin lessons laced with Cantonese

rebukes each time I blew a test or task;
Turkish on Wednesdays, and on Thursdays Persian;
Spanish on Fridays with a side of Basque;
early Venetian (the vernacular version)

Saturday afternoons, or else Punjabi,
whose musicality inflamed my stammer;
at night, a private language — just a hobby
till a French girl immersed me in its grammar;

Swedish, Swahili, Igbo, Uzbek, Wu;
Gaelic, in which I wrote a hopeless ode;
non-alphabetic symbol systems, too:
flag signals, the Victorian floral code,

birdcalls. I sought the key to all expression
in self-directed studies: music, math,
myth, mushrooms, Esperanto … Each digression
drove me half mad along its rambling path.

Beyond the vulgar elegance of English,
it seems my tourist tongue can only dabble.
On lonely shores, no longer young, still singlish,
I dream of all the smooth talk lost in Babel —

and of that ear in which I'll blurt someday
(in tones inflected possibly by Scotch)
the word that all the world burns to convey
and I'm still learning marvelous ways to botch.

FOR YOUR EYES ONLY

[Discovered in a locked drawer of the author's desk, which the author asked me to open in his absence. The filigreed key had been stashed in the hollow pommel of a walking stick. — Ed.]

The Secret of the House of Garamond.
If that is our real name.

The scream in the gazebo.
The beast in the boxwood.
The birdshit on the bust.

It rattles the dumbwaiter, upsets the vase.
Opens the hidden panel. Chills the pewter spoons.

Audit the library: it's logged in all the books.
The worm in the portfolio,
the tarnish on the frame.

All the rumors are true —
you are all our long-lost cousins or companions,
associates or intimates. The whole world knows,
which means we know why it must stay a secret.

The scratching in the basement.
The white slip at the window of the widow's watch.
The flaw in the eastern gable.

I scrawl it in the margin, tuck it in my breast pocket,
folding the paper six ways like the speech
that walled the bullet from a President's heart
(or walled it just enough).

My talisman. It will not let me go.
Of all my artifacts the most authentic,
it watches as I order one more wine
and order one more wine and guarantees
I'll be there in the morning.

NATURAL BORN

I.

I tried to fly, once, to my native land,
but Father pulled some strings and had me banned.
Sins of my youth revealed to some stern bureau…
I can't say more than that, but he was thorough.

"Visa denied for life," the agent said.
So I *absorbed* America instead:
mastered the spelling rules; spoke every word
with flattened vowels; casually referred
to "trucks"; became world-famous overnight;
wore ties whose stripes descended left to right;
failed to love rodeo and fries, but rallied,
not just because these preferences are valid
but because, luckily, the one credential
that renders all the others inessential —
thinking your problems pivotal to Earth —
had already been issued me at birth.

II.

You see your parents' point the more you learn…
Soon it seemed natural never to return.
Soon I moved on to new ways of rebelling
(except in my subconscious, and my spelling).

ENTER THE RIVAL

[Composed in unusually swift, emphatic penstrokes. — Ed.]

I.

I first disliked him during our third duel.
The fencing captain of the enemy school —

and, in our age group, champion of the nation —
he'd earned, in fact, my guarded admiration

right up until that match, that final tourney,
when he first played the prick. And spurred my journey.

He sauntered in as though he'd never lost.
As always when our paths and blades had crossed,

he never once removed his gray mesh mask.
(I've never found out why or cared to ask.)

As we squared off, he gestured heavenward
and chanted something solemn. Then: *En garde!*

My snowpea watched us from the topmost tier,
wielding her Gauloise (not the type to cheer

or heckle, either, only smoke and watch).
The first hit caught me right across the crotch.

Gasping, I knelt. The pain felt like a *buzz* —
a zap, a jolt of voltage. So it was:

the first of many nasty little shocks
to come. It seemed he'd rigged his signal box

to send a pulse of current to his sword
and through my nerve cells every time he scored.

He *had* scored, too. In modern smallsword duels,
below the belt is not against the rules.

Soon I had welts strewn all over my skin.
"Just a slight variation I threw in" —

he whispered when I lost — "to raise the stakes.
I get so tired of minor scrapes and aches!

Duels used to kill, you know? But you'll be fine.
Besides, I rigged your sword the same as mine."

II.

Later, as she massaged my back, I winced
and told her what he'd done. Less than convinced,

she eyed the markings on my flesh. *Perhaps*
they hurt so much, they only felt like zaps?

So cruel a prank — it hardly seems realistic.
To try it he would have to be — "Sadistic.

Yes." She kissed my shoulder. *Well, mon cher,*
unless he lied, at least the fight was fair.

"I ought to wring his neck." *Why so*, she said.
Why not an elegant revenge instead.

"Poison?" *Too elegant.* "Insulting poem?"
Ah, that would flatter him. I turned. "You know him?"

Her hands, which had been roving down my spine,
paused at my waist. *We had a glass of wine*

in Venice once — I told you, no? — with friends.
He is a bit — how do you say — intense.

From time to time he tries to correspond —
"Oh really." *Yes, but: Bladwell Garamond,*

since when have I returned a strange boy's letter?
Lie down. Relax. Undo your belt. That's better.

III.

He asked her, soon enough, to marry him.
It wasn't hard, that time, to parry him:

I laughed; she laughed; we read the notes he'd written
that week alone. Poor bastard, he was smitten.

Later he came back with a subtler thrust.
A passing, sidelong puncture of our trust —

slight twinge — small surface wound that failed to scab,
festered, then throbbed with an electric stab…

And yet the game goes on. The perfect rival
can be so vital to a love's survival.

Someday you'll tell your grandkids how you met
the enemy as one, held off the threat,

moved in a dance in which each touch was fire…
And even now I can't help but admire

his tactics, which I've come to know so well;
his stance, his *in quartata*, his *appel,*

his grace. His face I guess I'll see in hell.

III

WANDERLUST

ENTANGLEMENT

[Sent from a venerable spa in Zurich, in an envelope evidently loosened by steam. The attached note read: "Found this in my old hotel room safe. Wrote it for her many separations ago." — Ed.]

A fluid state,
as it was her prerogative to be,

a certain
classical uncertainty

wearing, on drumming fingers, orbital rings,
taking a smoke break outside space and time

(to measure her to miss her —
even to attempt —
even the instruments shrug, *Je ne sais quoi*);

nor was she, at the borderline, detained
by the gendarme of her own reflexive Frenchness:
she slipped between the Pyrenees
as through guitar strings
into the Spanish tense
where the noon is long
and the siesta's dream contains all times at once;
became the mood, the tone,
the very substance of the *subjuntivo*,
which every lover longs toward … In the zone
of nontranslation, meanwhile, I remained

both coming and going.
Schrödinger's affair.

I miss her. That is
neither here nor there.

BLAD, POSTGRAD

Decisions, decisions.
I didn't make them, but I made my way —
from Bath to Bangkok, Bern and back again.

I printed hundreds of blank business cards
and tossed them one by one into the Seine,
which hired me to stare at it six hours a day
(my wages images, my colleagues pigeons).

My personal funds had long since sprung a leak.
I rode on credit spun from sheer mystique.

Down byways, autobahns, and boulevards
I drove my '58 Mongoose Civique:
a crow-blue roadster with white racing stripes
and nickel trimmings, fitted with secret gears,
circular rearview mirror, fawn-brown seats,
a dashboard lighter customized for pipes,
and, in the glove box, an homage to Keats
that moved a traffic constable to tears…

The real world unprepared for me — birds winging it, trees
startled into greenness as I disembarked,
tarmacs unscrolling, backroads rolling till I parked
and watched the whole scene freeze.

I couldn't get away with it for long,
or be away from her. But what to *be*?

Or more precisely, do? Write poetry?
A poet is anyone who has a strong
opinion about the moon — and I had three,
and she'd heard all of them, and called them wrong.

INCIDENT AT SEA

To tell the anguish that abounds therein,
The language of my tongue cannot begin.
But 'list unto me and I will here explain,
The course to steer…

— W. M. Murrell, "Explanation," *Map on Temperance*

Of all my fears, the worst is that I'll choke.
God, what an ignominious way to die!
You feel your throat catch as if *you* are caught
inside the closing walls of some sick joke;
your eyes start welling up — you want to cry —
you've botched the first thing you were ever taught!

I know whereof I speak. I was aboard
my boat one night, accompanied by a drink.
With one last absent swig I gulped the garnish,
only to swallow, too, the tiny sword
it had been speared with … I began to sink.
I hit the deck and smelled the dizzying varnish.

I had no brave last words, no gasp of air
with which to conjure some, no crew amid
whose closing ranks I might soliloquize —
no parting shot, no prophecy, no prayer.
Then something massive (hammerhead or squid)
walloped the boat, which threatened to capsize,

but only tipped so sharply that I slammed
against the port rail with fantastic force.

The sword flew out and struck the wooden mast —
it stuck there like an arrow. "I'll be damned,"
I breathed. I leapt up, got the boat on course,
and poured another drink, and not my last…

All of which is to say, I don't fear death
(which, whether slow or sudden, whether dealt
by pirate or by pushpin, must entail
somehow the awkwardness of loss of breath);
I fear sheer carelessness. The *fault* I felt —
knowing my words, at last, deserved to fail.

THE RIDE

*[Author's note: "Memory of a reunion after our first separation."
— Ed.]*

That night in June.
The hilltop,
the gliding moon,
the riding crop.

The horses' tethers taut
where they'd been tied.
The wine we'd brought
to liven up the ride.

Her kneecap slightly bruised —
"Let me massage that."
How lightly she refused.
Her black dressage hat,

shadbelly, vest.
The view: the valley, the village.
Wine on her buttoned breast
in sudden spillage

and the spill mopped
by my hand's soft brush.
My blush. The hill topped
with a moss like plush.

My face in it.
Her body on my back,

stripped down in one split
second. The whip crack.

Her gartered thighs,
her clipped commands,
my muffled cries,
her white-gloved hands,

the quirt
the crop
the hurt
“Don’t stop — ”

Clouds torn apart
as if by chariots.
Raw dawn. A heart
like Secretariat’s.

GARAMOND'S FIRST THEOREM

...a truly marvelous proof...
— Fermat

Sorbonne professor, Royal Society Fellow,
doyenne with chalk poised like a cigarette,
she strode onstage to wild applause at lectures
and played the chalkboard like a violincello.
She knocked off Theorems, nailed down Conjectures
(some of which hadn't been Conjectured yet),
earned endowed chairs and Erdős number 3,
and, in spare moments, tried to tutor me.

Lounging in bed one night, we wrote a paper
touching upon the cosmological constant.
— She did, I mean. I was her faithful helper:
polishing notes, smiling with satellite glow,
technically earning Erdős number 4,
riding a surge of insight for one instant
before it merged into the cosmic flow...
Jotting vague margin comments. Promising more.

OPIUM DREAM

I came suddenly upon such knotty problems of alleys, such enigmatical entries, and such sphynx's riddles of streets without thoroughfares...

— Thomas De Quincey,
Confessions of an English Opium-Eater

The fog of alleyways, the plaza's blur,
the sputter of motors, the propeller's whirr,
the radio's ballad fastening like a burr
or chip implanted by some saboteur
deep in the brain cells' weave — all these concur
with each bribed captain, cabman, and chauffeur:
the paths of the labyrinth lead back to Her.

Signs in the lobby, verses of *Les Fleurs*
du mal (in all translations), the snarling of a cur
trapped on a rooftop and the housecat's purr
twined with the syntax of the chat-show chatterer —
all these confirm, as if you still weren't sure:
the world's clandestine messages refer
to one big in-joke with the punchline *Her*.

Drown it in music, drown it in liqueur
or coffee, smoke whichever herbs deter
or grains diffuse the bad moon; let the dream recur —
bid shadows fall and walls begin to slur
and the strum strum strum of a compulsive dulcimer
pollute your ear canals till that last pure,
non-toxic, tonic chord rings out: brings
HER.

MR. GARAMOND WEEPS

A little room devoted to the purpose.
Couch green and gold, like Keats's cot in Rome.
Thick curtains drawn. Door barred. Do not disturb us:
we are not at home.

I shoot my cuffs, remove the studs of pearl,
place tie pin, collar stiffeners, signet ring
in notches of a baize-lined case, set fob
and watch down tenderly, let down the spring,
undo my tie, suppress a minor sob,
shed my suit piece by piece, sort, fold, and furl,
and lay the neat stack on a nearby chair.

Shake out my pocket square.
Place it in easy reach. (She used to fold the silk
into a dove, complete with tiny beak.)
Adjust a violet nodding on its stalk.

I am standing in one sock…

Now I am facedown, laid out on the cot
as if sewn into it. I clutch it like a child
I once saw riding a dog around a field.
I shake it, but the best antiques don't break…

some kind of joke some kind of sick mistake
she's gone she's gone she's gone she's gone she's not
here not with me somewhere with him right now

fuck fuck fuck fuck fuck fuck fuck fuck fuck fuck
fuck let it not be true let him be struck
dead let my suffering summon her somehow
you mean the way her suffering summoned you
all right all right but but but but but what
my throbbing head my ribs my sobs my snot
my nakedness this shaking cot they'll pass
they'll pass this ugly room will pass you too
you stupid ass. You ass. You ass. You ass.

Wobbling a little, Mr. Garamond stands.
I step back into him. Put pants on. Tuck
tails into waistband, wind my pendant watch,
retie my tie, relink my cufflinks, pluck
each collar stiffener from its plush green notch,
slide each in place, reproach my shaking hands,
make of my sob-soaked, snot-soaked pocket square
a goddamned peacock, and walk out of there.

CHANSON

Drunken nights
call back at once all other drunken nights.
A chain of floating islands, linked by secret doors.
Dream logic mixed like cocktails, metaphors.

Anyone could recur,
like good or evil luck.
(Is that my piano teacher in the hammock?)
Historical figures: the astronomer
with the golden nose, who died of holding it in.
(My bladder tugging at my sleeve again.)

She could walk in. She might.
If on my fifth drink at the stroke of midnight
I make a wish upon a slice of lime
and say her name, she'll be here in no time.

Draped in Chantilly lace
and singing torch songs — orchid on her shoulder,
smoke in her voice, cigarette in her holder.
Glimmer of recognition on her face.

WAYLAID

> *On the floor she found a belt and a buckle which she sent to Genji next day with a complicated acrostic poem in which she compared these stranded properties to the weeds which after their straining and tugging the waves leave upon the shore.*
>
> — Murasaki Shikibu, *The Tale of Genji*

Shipwrecked again. I disentangled kelp
from belt loops, collar, cuffs. Soon I had help:

a willowy woman, nearly seven feet,
out for a seaside stroll. A scholar of myth
who'd combed the Aeolian Islands, Cyprus, Crete,
foothills and arid footnotes, gathering shards
of the existence of forgotten bards.

Her island had an unrecorded name
and stony coast. The villa she shared with
twelve pampered kittens smelled of sweet botanicals;
her bed was spacious with a silver frame
and, dangling from the posts, four iron manacles.

Her tone was docent-smooth throughout the tour.
"We'll rest," she said, "and then I'll show you more."

We picnicked on the lawn, drank hyacinth wine,
smoked lettuce, lotus, opium, catnip, cloves;
splashed one another, laughing, in the coves —
and when she shed the dress I'd soaked with brine,
I stared and stared, my brain completely lotused.
I stayed and stayed. Weeks floated by unnoticed.

Or else months, years … I can't exactly say
she held me there with whips or chains or potions.
Held me unwillingly, I mean. Pure play
in all its strangely regulated motions
secured our bondage, while the unloosed forces
lashing her little rock with wind and foam
brought gorgeous seabirds, tortoises, seahorses
weaving their spell of charm about the game.
It worked, most days. But even where no home
or love lies waiting (only more chains, more locks),
allegiance to the kingdom of the Previous
will render every fresh devotion devious
and every clawed adventure deadly tame.

I bolted. Grabbed a rowboat by the oarlocks.
Twelve kittens bristled at me, pupils narrowing.
I threw them back a wounded look. Escape?
No, no — the shedding of a false belief.
I launched my vessel with a headlong scrape
and splash; missed, by a whisker's breadth, the reef
toward which a new sail was already arrowing.

As for supplies, I'd smuggled out enough
to scrub my tender limbs, conceal each faint
mark of resistance with a linen cuff,
mix a dark cocktail in a salt-rimmed cup,
and toast the sail as my clear brain whipped up
an unrecorded epic of restraint.

GENEVIÈVE'S VERSION

[One afternoon, without warning and with only the lightest of knocks, Mme Sans-Serif appeared in my office. From her small black bag she produced a tape machine and pressed Record. Perching on the windowsill, she began to reminisce, only to cut herself off after five minutes. She sighed and left. Days later, she sent me a transcript of her statement, versified with minimal changes to the original. — Ed.]

The secret name
my family gave to me,
the streets from which we came,
how long I spied
and on which side
and in what war
(if it was even real) —
all this and more
I am at liberty
not to reveal.

As Garamond
found out. Unhappy man!
Of such frustration
he has grown so fond.
Bold captain without plan
still drifting on,
still adding all the globe,
nation by nation,
to his grand wardrobe
of accoutrements.

His pipe, you know.
A man who smokes to savor.

Prefers his suicide
scented and slow —
leans back, takes pains
to register the flavor
of each sun-dried,
lovingly chosen leaf…
Life is too brief!
I smoke in furious chains.

Our little jokes,
you know. Well, one could take
a stick of chalk
and with a few quick strokes,
some smiles, some clever talk,
prove how our break
occurred, show why it must
in every case,
boom-boom, erase
the board, wave off the dust —

and what would be solved then?
Some days, one tires
of men in the abstract,
of all the loopholes men
slip through, but not the way
a scent, or else
some quiet fact —
how do you say? — conspires,
that is, compels…
Perhaps, you do not say.

SUPERFLUOUS MAN

Might he not be, in fact, a parody?
— Pushkin, *Eugene Onegin*

Here like a man in traction I lie sprawling
with one foot propped up on a blood-red sofa.
My heel imprints the arm. A tasseled loafer
hangs from my toetips on the verge of falling.

A warm draft fills the room. The tassel stirs.
I watch its quiet writhing with dispassion.
Outside, the clouds drift in and out of fashion.
My lover's flown away. The sofa's hers.

My nails are nubs, worn by compulsive buffing
amid perpetual dreams of her beside me
stroking my brow, or roughhousing astride me
until the cushions burst with horsehair stuffing.

Stains in the armpits of my silk pajamas
expand, expand … I'm everything I've dreaded:
one long quotation awkwardly embedded,
gripped in the clawed tongs of inverted commas

from my first jabbering to my last faint terror.
How many of me can the copier copy
before the ink runs low, the job grows sloppy,
even the hope of some unusual error

diminishes to blankness? … Heirloom portraits
gloat from the far wall, whispering: *To live*

is to be painfully derivative.
Why pout about it? Were you hoping your *traits*

would turn out to be more than ours restored?
That they were just so many "self-made riches"?
A horsehair slips into my shirt and itches.
I scratch. My nail-nubs bleed. I am not bored:

her ghostly image lingers, still engrossing.
In her dark eyes I was original once —
at least, I felt a twinge of renaissance…
Till I collapsed into this mode of posing,

arranged my life and limbs in this grand flop.
I sweat, I itch … How long will one pose hold
before the body gives up, or grows old?
The tassel stirs. The loafer does not drop.

DISTRESS

[Composed after the author's fourth separation from Mme Sans-Serif ("the only one I ever initiated"). Transmitted via marine radio and intercepted by the Fijian Navy. Decrypted. Declassified. Forwarded to my office. — Ed.]

Stargazing starboard, darling. Steadily heading
west toward my destination: Micronesia.
(Even the name sounds like a small forgetting.
Albeit fleeting.) Free but not at leisure.
Pacing the poop by moonlight. Stooping to play
euchre over the gunwale with the porpoises.
Losing. The game, my mind. (Too much sea spray
makes minds, like shipboards, tend to warp as is.)
Recovering. Reading, by St. Elmo's fire,
a nineteenth-century allegorical map:
Temptation Straits, the Happiness Empire
lurking along the bottom like a trap…

May my heart raise, the day I reach that shore,
a little white surrender semaphore.

IV

INTERLUDE

EDITOR'S CAVEAT

Pardon my intrusion. I do not wish to disrupt.

Each time I comment, in fact, it is with the feeling of tracking mud into a temple or shouting, "My hemorrhoids — " just as the party falls silent.

Pardon me again. I will strike that line in proofs.

I wish to inform the reader that, in the course of editing this project, I received an anonymous letter. It began: "The rich are different from you and me. Except when they aren't." It urged me to investigate the principal figures in Mr. Garamond's memoir, hinting that "one of them is, so to speak, touring on false passports." Enclosed was advice on observing high society incognito, along with enough money to facilitate the mission.

As this was a fact-checking assignment, I accepted.

My research determined that the letter is correct: one of the three principals is an interloper of sorts, though perhaps less a fraud than a fellow mole. I will say no more at this time. There are considerations here beyond the editorial.

Now to return to the story. Once again, pardon my intervention.

FORTUNE

Each time I tried to give it all away,
it came back threefold. Dogged me like a hex.
My uncle's neighbor willed me his Monet.
The orphanage wordlessly returned my checks.

Currency changed, but never lost its smell.
Greenback and lira, dram, dinar, and rand
weathered all climates as they rose and fell,
but drew the same perfume across my hand.

Rupee and ruble, Tanzanian shilling —
I didn't ask for them and didn't earn them.
Each time I buried them, I made a killing.
The match blew out each time I tried to burn them.

Always my coat and collar wore their smell.
I squandered vast sums at Chemin de Fer,
woke in the finest suite of my hotel,
opened the safe and found the whole wad there.

Pounds left in pubs on rainy afternoons,
motley Bahamian dollars, pale blue yen,
obsolete coinage — oboli, doubloons —
flowed underground and home to me again.

Florin and peso and Icelandic krona:
all breathed a scent no distance would dispel.
The fortune left no haven for its owner.
Sheltered in vaults or in an offshore "shell,"

exchanged in liquid, frictionless transaction
for francs in Switzerland or Senegal,
or dematerialized into abstraction —
typed as a floating mark, ideal *real*,

pure glowing token to acquire or sell —
the money kept, through each disguise or screen,
the sweetly desperate, densely human smell
no wishing-well will ever quite wash clean.

THE UNACKNOWLEDGED

[Composed anonymously on yellow legal paper and delivered via courier. Asked whether he had written it, Mr. Garamond shook his head. Asked whether I should publish it, he slowly nodded. — Ed.]

I practice law wherever I can practice.
I partner fluidly with countless firms.
I, like my rival, live on my own terms.
It's fair to say that similar things attract us.

I grant you, mine's the less exalted trade —
the more despised, yes — but the final line
of every book is dotted, and is mine.
Mine are the words of which the world is made.

In "legalese" (a term I do not care for),
in the hermetic tongue all earthly tribes
assign to faceless ranks of harried scribes
heaving an unheard sigh with every "Wherefore";

in language neither fanciful nor factual,
in prose that specifies but does not *mean* —
denser than Kant and ten times more obscene
than the most lurid curse — in cool, contractual,

intricate clauses, itemized conditions,
I implement (or else compose) those laws
that seem to have the cosmos as their cause.
My sweetest triumph lies in my omissions.

I leave my private stamp on wills and deeds,
divorces, plea deals, petty litigation,
amended drafts of prominent legislation,
and fine print no sane person ever reads.

My powers could place my rival in a cell;
could, in a flash, cost him his house, his boat,
his clothes, his name — for what it's worth, his vote —
but I prefer to see him pace that hell

he has inherited. Oh, I know each
pitfall, each snare his privileges entail;
the point at which his best defense will fail;
the hidden source of his internal breach —

but knowledge isn't action. Or intent.
Meanwhile he keeps the fight up, files his long
complaint against a world that's done him wrong...
This world. My world. The thing I represent.

V

TROUBLE WITHIN TROUBLE

L'ORIGINE III: THE SAGA BEGINS

*The rack or single foot or running walk (*tölt*) is the distinctive gait of the Icelandic horse, setting it apart from other European breeds. It is for taking it easy over smooth ground … The pace (*skeid*) is used for short stretches at high speed.*

— Sigurður A. Magnússon, *The Iceland Horse*

In the first century, the sagas say,
a king named Bladvald — known as The Impaler —
held all of Iceland in his savage sway.
Charts of the north sea warned the wandering sailor.

He wielded crushing force by force of habit,
speared whales for sport and couldn't get his fill,
no sooner saw a landmass but would grab it,
and from each glacier-side proclaimed his will.

Torches grew pale before his burning beard;
the palace mirrors swore he was immortal.
Next to his wrath his children chiefly feared
his jagged smile and fjord-blooded chortle.

Horses he'd stolen from his hapless foes
grew coarser coats and learned the alien grace
of two new gaits upon his native snows:
one called the *tölt* and one the *flying pace*.

Foaming with drink, he ran down to attack
the mocking ocean, mad to overwhelm it
once and for all … The breakers beat him back
until his skull rang like an iron helmet.

His gleaming eyes grew dark pits underneath;
his feet succumbed to bunions and to gout;
years of sweet mead at meals despoiled his teeth;
a hernia left him permanently stout.

Men of unmelting heart and gleaming eye,
of mind berserk and confidence unbridled —
sure of who wounded them, and how, and why,
and to what world of vengeance they're entitled —

all fall beneath the same wave, the same way.
One night the king lay snoring, and forthwith
his mildest daughter, so the sagas say
(though who can chart where memory turns to myth),

crept to his room, forgave him with a dagger,
sped from the palace at the flying pace
astride a shaggy little steed named Bragr,
and fled across the snow without a trace.

MR. GARAMOND'S AMERICAN DREAM

[Composed near dawn in a bedside journal. — Ed.]

At last my preparations went as planned.
I foiled the final bureaucratic scheme.
I filed the forms that would unlock the land
alleged to feature in the world's own dream.

I sailed off, whistling, into soundless fog.
It blurred my course. I cursed it as I drifted,
gulped down self-pity like a bitter grog,
and glimpsed the shore before the shroud had lifted.

My ghost ship landed on a solid shelf;
I joined a queue and gave a guard my permit;
he saw at first glance that I was myself,
but ducked into a back room to confirm it.

Ice cream and salted nuts at corner stands…
A gritty grandeur close enough to taste…
The guard came back extending empty hands.
"I'm very sorry, sir. It's been misplaced."

"You mean the country? Look in there," I joked,
gesturing toward the spires behind the mist.
He frowned: "I'm sorry, sir. It's been revoked.
We've had to place you on the permanent list."

"Of what?" "Of foreign visitors who lack
the proper — " "But you stole it!" "Sir, I wish you'd

watch how you speak — " "I wish you'd give it back."
"I'm sorry, sir, but it was never issued."

I drew out all the papers from my coat:
"Won't you just read these?" I'd begun to whine.
He glanced and laughed. "You came on your own boat?
Why don't you sail on home, sir. You'll be fine."

"This *is* home," I protested. "I was born
to parents traveling — " "Buddy, what's the game?"
His accent nicely accented his scorn.
"No way that horseshit's even your real name."

The spires dissolved. The land slipped out of sight.
My prow went nosing into unseen regions.
I lay down on the deck, rose late at night,
stared at the fog, and calmly pledged allegiance.

THE TIME TRAVELS OF BLAD J. GARAMOND

A homemade rig based on a Renaissance sketch
and certain files I stole from Copenhagen.
A quantum-oscillating, bat-winged wagon
fully equipped for four-dimensional flight:
twin engines, shiny knobs, logbook, gearbox,
a small receptacle in which to retch,
shields to prevent a temporal paradox
(the past may not be touched; Dickens was right)...

Hand on the gearshift, I reviewed my reasons.
To see my private history, of course
(but not the future, even if I'd dared:
the necessary highway's not yet built);
to retrace fragrant memories to their source,
fix names and dates to my free-floating guilt...
To go back further, too, and not be spared.
To see. To be, in some sense, "for all seasons."

I pressed a button. Eminent guests, assembled
in my home laboratory, cheered. Time trembled.

My audience must have seen me disappear
and rematerialize the following moment.
They backed away, too petrified to comment,
as the door cracked and, in a fog of stench,
my eyes fixed forward and my clothing stale,
I staggered past them (shoes oozing a trail)

and stretched out flat across a window-bench,
where I lay frozen for what seemed a year.

My doctor spoke. I bolted up in terror.
I managed presently to understand him.
"Where did you set the dial?" he cried. "Which era?"
"Childhood," I whispered. "Then the war. Then Random."
He scratched his beard. "You didn't interact…?"
I waved a weary hand: "It's all intact."
"I see." He seemed relieved. "What happened, then?"
I chuckled tonelessly. "To whom? And when?
All of it happened. I just watched it pass
in little segments — shards — never intruded —
caused nothing, changed nothing — myself included —
was nothing — sat there — lurked behind the glass,
you know: the perfect tourist, perfect phantom —
watching. Sometimes again. Ha ha: 'again.'"
"I see." The doctor coughed. He touched my brow
and packed his bag. "Well, it's all over now."

There the rig stood against the brightening wall:
twin engines dead, wings pitifully sprained,
shields operational but faded, drained
of tint, as if they knew the things they'd seen.
The logbook entries were a childish scrawl.
The puke container was the whole machine.

THE SPACE TRAVELS OF BLAD J. GARAMOND

Finally I searched for her on other planets.
Applying her cosmology and my own cosmetic touches,
I built a small craft that could do the job —
could putter, at least, around the local superclusters.
I lit the thrusters and my pipe. Liftoff.

Back the world shrank, blue pupil against black,
constricting in the circular rearview. Then:
blank dark. The medium through which hearts sink
made general. Solar systems sinking in it.

That is the truth, that space between the stars:
it isn't nothing, absence, or a void,
since there it is and there you are. It's just
a confirmation of correct proportion;
your lenses jettison their last distortion . . .

You lose your bearings across all dimensions.
You lose your mind, whose lodestar is a flame
snuffed by a lighter-lid light years ago.

I wandered through the whole trichiliocosm,
adapting to all climates, adopting all manner of manners,
encountering convicts, politicians, sentries
pointing with tentacles which way she'd gone;
at long last scrambling up the battered slope
of some galactic Matterhorn, convinced

I’d find her at the peak…discovering, instead,
bare rock. The jeweled abysm overhead.
A zodiac bright and senseless as my hope.

JOUISSANCE

Once in a wardrobe full of silk and sable —
once in the corner of a Warmblood's stable —

often along the Laugavegur Trail,
in tarpaulin shelters under pelting hail —

out on the moors, as if to tempt pneumonia —
above the canopy of Amazonia —

with that geologist we knew in Soho,
beneath a photograph of Pu'u 'Ō'ō —

dressed for your bacchanals, a feathered freak —
behind a hotel bar in Mozambique —

on Innisfree, among a choir of linnets —
inside Big Ben for twenty deafening minutes —

aboard abandoned ships from fore to aft,
taffrail to fo'c'sle to inflated raft,
tied in the rigging, chained in the engine room,
perched on the far tip of the flying jib-boom —

inside the Louvre at night — inside my mind —
inside a gondola (the ski lift kind) —

through rain and snow and seasons off the charts
I loved you — felt your love in fits and starts —

and sank back into dim rooms where we sighed
for all the passing whims we'd satisfied.

DISSOLUTION CLAUSE

[One pleasant summer in the Azores, Mr. Garamond and Mme Sans-Serif were moved to form a prenuptial agreement. After a long delay, the law firm Mr. Garamond retained drew up the following document, which departed substantially from his requests. — Ed.]

1. All of these terms and time's own laws
shall be negated by this clause;

1.1. And if that clause should cause distress,
this clause shall guarantee redress;

1.2. And if, pursuant to the above,
redress comes in the form of love
that soon enough brings unfulfillment,
this clause shall guarantee annulment;

1.3. And if redress in the form of wealth
should be reclaimed by force or stealth,
this clause shall faithfully restore
the lack that rankled less before;

1.4. And if redress in the form of knowledge
nauseates, this clause shall abolish
all but the absolute awareness
of Earth's personal unfairness;

1.5. And if redress in the form of power
fails to last a billable hour,
this clause faithfully reaffirms
the power that voids all time and terms.

REHEARSAL

[Composed during a hiatus in the run of one of Mr. Garamond's theatricals. — Ed.]

My changing room. My own face floating nearer.
The frame of naked bulbs around the mirror.
The motley console of the makeup kit;
its range and depth as I stare into it,

breathing its cool perfume. The brilliant hues
staring back as if daring me to choose,
tonight, to blur the contours of my role.
Truly redo myself. The sponge, the bowl.

The kohl-black pencil, keen to emphasize
boldly the dubious eyes that meet my eyes
and peer and frown as if to diagnose.
The glass. The open case. The face up close —

complexion dry or oily, smooth or pitted;
blemishes well-disguised or unadmitted;
upper lip stiff or quivering, shaved or stubbled;
forehead engraved or outwardly untroubled;

foundation, shadow, blush, concealer, cream;
the wish to be or not be as we seem;
the ways in which it may or may not matter;
illusions that the softest brush won't flatter;

powder and gel, emollient and emulsion,
accent and underline; the heart's compulsion

to heighten what defines us; our contrasting
rash of revulsion at the world's typecasting;

our amateurish blending, like the actor
making the best of things before Max Factor —
testing out mercury and lard and lead;
the fear that change may leave us scarred or dead;

the fear that sameness will arrest us, hackneyed,
in some forgotten pageant — paint our acne'd
features with shame that won't be swabbed away
or wash our gladness to a permanent gray;

what can't be saved by atmosphere and lighting
or lacquered with the glaze of clever writing;
whatever stray hairs or unstraightened teeth
survive — whatever hives break out beneath

regimes of beauty, codes of hue and shade,
modes of performance whose long empires fade
or melt and slide away like flakes of grease
from a cracked skull collapsing piece by piece;

all that the burning bulbs seem to embellish,
mapping a landscape — broad and bright and hellish —
behind the glass now close enough to kiss
if one did not repel oneself . . . all this

I take in frankly: they've tacked up a new list:
my life's recast: I never was the duelist
gallantly tearing off his mask of mesh
and baring to the crowd his unscathed flesh;

or else the rugged villain, suave amour,
sidekick or page or Peddler Number Four;
mine is the shtick of which you're never rid,
and there's no show tonight. I close the lid

on tones that span the entire human scale
plus those of petals and the peacock's tail.
The glass dismisses me. Still blankly drawn,
I exit through the back door. I go on.

"IF ANY OF YOU KNOW CAUSE..."

Reader, you'll have already guessed this part:
the doubtful ushers glancing at the skies;
the clouds uniting darkly, brooding, showering;
bride and groom fleeing the same jinxed marriage
at the same time (she with a brief head start),
then winding up in the same railway carriage,
wearing the same black duster as disguise —
meanwhile the groomsmen grim, the bridesmaids glowering,
the violinist mystified, the towering
rococo cake collapsing at its heart.

VI

SOUVENIRS

EDITOR'S POSTSCRIPT

For months, I had no word from Mr. Garamond. Correspondence foundered at each of his addresses; a courier informed me that his cottage had been demolished. With nothing more to read or proof, no other pressing tasks over the summer, I took long lunchtime walks along the shore.

One afternoon, at the end of the stone jetty near my office, I spied a bottle of Beaujolais bobbing in the waves. Uncorking it, I found a sheaf of pensées by Mme Sans-Serif. The margins were dense with penciled graphs, the pages foxed and flecked with drops of purple.

One week later — I had checked religiously in the interim — a second bottle turned up at the jetty. Inside was a poem in the typeface I knew well, attached to a note in Mr. Garamond's hand: "Driven here and there by the zephyrs of restlessness. May still have a chance with her. More soon, I hope."

I waited dutifully the following week. This time, the message in a bottle was a ship in a bottle: a perfect replica of the Geneviève, *down to her name hand-painted on the hull. Its sails were furled, its anchor dropped, its mainmast crowned with a miniature white flag.*

I was seized by an urge to dash it on the rocks. Staying my hand just in time, I cradled the bottle, stared out over the waves, and whispered, "Stet."

THE PENSÉES OF GENEVIÈVE SANS-SERIF

A romance is a conspiracy about which the conspirators themselves can only theorize.

Δ

No matter how passionately a writer embraces you, he is winking over your shoulder at posterity.

Δ

The dream of an afterlife is the fear of commitment.

Δ

This wager of Pascal's! This trust in Power to honor obligations! A bankrupt house cannot reward the gambler; an omnipotent house can smile and renege. *For your own good...*

Δ

The poet labors to convey a flower's charms. But what is her labor in French to the woman who knows only Dutch? The flower itself has no such problem.

Δ

Therefore, art constructed from natural language is justified not by universalities but by particularities. That is, peculiarities ... This has been said elsewhere. I am craving a cigarette.

Δ

Mathematics: a language for those who wish to be comprehensible everywhere and comprehended nowhere.

Δ

Reason has a heart, of which the heart knows nothing.

Δ

Just as the rich get richer, the loved attract more love.

Δ

Writers make difficult lovers, less because of their chemical addictions than because of their addiction to revision. It is a short step from discarding and rewriting poetry to destroying and rebuilding romance. The goal in each case is the same annoying illusion: "It came to me all at once." "It was love at first sight."

Δ

We do not want to drink so much as drink to want.

Δ

Rimbaud: *Je est un autre*. Jiménez: *Yo no soy yo*. That is: I ≠ I. How often poets claim this and how seldom spies do! *Identity* of course is different to the mathematician, to the lawyer ... We are accountable to our definitions. The lawyer less so.

Rimbaud stopped making such claims when he became an exporter. That is, a smuggler...

Δ

I know very well what I want. I want my desire to vary.

Δ

How distressing to man is woman, who so often ignores his sex. How much more distressing is the woman mathematician, who so often ignores his species.

Δ

"Man," "woman" — an approximation, a problem of definition. The solution: not to attempt. I am suddenly very hungry.

Δ

Truly variable desire would not vary at a constant rate. There would be lovers whom we desire for long periods, long but unpredictable ... Perhaps one we desire for so long that variation seems to end...

Δ

Lady Lovelace: "I am more than ever now the bride of science."

Δ

Soon there will be a pill to curb all appetites, all addictions. The makers will not take it: they must maximize their profits.

Δ

Of the lover to whom I return most, what can I say? What tempts me back? I think it is the quality of our arguments.

CECI N'EST PAS

This picture's not a pipe.
That actor's not a king.
Shadows aren't anything.
Wax fruit is never ripe,

no matter how well made
or how hungry the sculptor.
It can't be peeled or pulped or
turned to lemonade.

I'm sorry to inform you:
even the steamiest scene
on the most glowing screen
won't substantively warm you.

All that I scrawl across
this treacherous blank space
fails to be your sweet face.
This is not a loss.

The End

PALINODE

APPREHENDED. — A local man living under the name "Blad J. Garamond" and claiming to be the heir of a London finance mogul was arrested today on charges of fraud, forgery, imposture, obscenity, blasphemy, malfeasance, misfeasance, nonfeasance, malpractice, petty larceny, grand larceny, medium larceny, misappropriation, public intoxication, counterfeiting, smuggling, criminal mischief, lèse-majesté, espionage, negligence, and horse theft. As police took the suspect into custody, a reporter from the Mirror *asked what his real name was and whether he had any regrets. The suspect was heard to say, "My name is Regret."*

A NOTE ON THE TYPES

Avenir is the masterpiece of Swiss designer Adrian Frutiger, who called it "the most precise typeface I've ever drawn." One of the more popular geometric sans-serif fonts, it manages "to encompass all the present fashions" while living up to its name, the French for *future*. Musing on the difference between serif and sans-serif types, Frutinger once observed that "they're two different worlds. The one world is that of the softer, rounder typefaces for poetry and literature. The other is that of the sober, clear typefaces for signage and information. … [I]n a serif typeface you can hide your mistakes; use the serifs to fudge things, or the junctures. In contrast, the sans serif is like a slippery eel, always sliding through your fingers, it's very difficult to get a grip on it." Nevertheless, Frutinger took pride in Avenir's "strict construction," which heightens rather than undermines its "humanist appearance." The intent behind his design was simple: "I just wanted to bring a bit of humanity to the field of geometric types."

Garamond derives from the work of sixteenth-century French punchcutter, publisher, and type designer Claude Garamont. ("Garamond" is a posthumous corruption of the name.) In *Type Lore: Popular Fonts of Today, Their Origin and Use; the History of the Art of Typography Succinctly Related for Practical Men*, J. L. Frazier writes: "The swash characters lend considerable variety to a Garamond composition. The capitals slope at different angles and when set with lower-case suggest a measure of restlessness." Of the designer, Frazier remarks: "[His] importance…and his part in the development of printing is firmly established. Little, however, is known regarding Garamond." Misattributions have clouded his legacy, as Paul Beaujon laments: "It would seem that Garamont's name, having so long been used on a design he never cut, is now by stern justice left off the face which is undoubtedly his." Most sources agree that Garamont worked in Paris, struggled financially, and married twice. He is not known to have fathered any children.

ABOUT THE AUTHOR

Austin Allen is the author of *Pleasures of the Game* (Waywiser Books), winner of the Anthony Hecht Poetry Prize. He has worked as an editor at Abbeville Press and as a writing instructor at Johns Hopkins University, the University of Cincinnati, and Emerson College. He currently teaches writing and literature at the University of the Virgin Islands.

www.ingramcontent.com/pod-product-compliance
Lightning Source LLC
Chambersburg PA
CBHW020612310726
48979CB00008B/1443/J

* 9 7 8 1 9 3 9 5 7 4 4 1 1 *